THE MONARCH BUTTERFLY

BY
JUDITH PINKERTON JOSEPHSON

EDITED BY
JUDY LOCKWOOD

PUBLISHED BY
CRESTWOOD HOUSE
Mankato, MN, U.S.A.

LIBRARY OF CONGRESS CATALOGING IN PUBLICATION DATA

Josephson, Judith Pinkerton.
 The monarch butterfly

 (Wildlife, habits & habitat)
 Includes index.
 SUMMARY: Examines the physical characteristics, behavior, lifestyle,
migration, and natural environment of the monarch butterfly.
 1. Monarch butterfly—Juvenile literature. [1. Monarch butterfly. 2.
Butterflies] I. Lockwood, Judy. II. Title. III. Series.
QL561.D3J67   1988   595.78'9   88-10871
ISBN 0-89686-389-1

International Standard Book Number:	Library of Congress Catalog Card Number:
0-89686-389-1	88-10871

PHOTO CREDITS:

Cover: DRK Photo: John Gerlach
DRK Photo: (Dwight R. Kuhn) 12; (John Gerlach) 14;
  (D. Cavagnaro) 25; (Jeff Foott) 33; (Stephen J. Krasemann) 37
Tom Stack & Associates: (Don & Esther Phillips) 4, 26; (Rod Planck) 8;
  (Jeff Foott) 17, 38, 41; (John Gerlach) 18; (Hal Clason) 20; (John
  Shaw) 22, 28, 29, 30, 31, 32; (Ken W. Davis) 11

Produced by Carnival Enterprises.

CRESTWOOD HOUSE

Box 3427, Mankato, MN, U.S.A. 56002

TABLE OF CONTENTS

The monarch butterfly is a familiar sight throughout North America and other parts of the world.

INTRODUCTION:

The monarch is one of the most familiar butterflies in the world. It is found throughout North America and parts of other continents. Seeing the monarch's colorful orange, black, and white-dotted wings fluttering overhead brings to mind the beauty and magic of all butterflies.

Like other butterflies, the monarch changes forms

as it grows—from egg to larva, pupa, and adult. People might see the monarch as a fat, green-and-black-striped caterpillar crawling on a milkweed leaf. Or they may glimpse the shimmering green monarch chrysalis (pronounced CHRIS-a-lis) (the hard shell covering the pupa) hanging from a twig. Usually, people see the monarch as an adult butterfly, fluttering, gliding, dipping, and darting among the flowers.

This delicate-looking butterfly is actually a powerful flier. Each fall, it flies hundreds of miles from summer homes in the north to warmer wintering spots in the south. Huge flocks of monarchs cling together by the thousands on trees, looking like bright, velvety leaves. In the spring, the monarchs fly north again, laying eggs as they go.

The migration of the monarch is amazing and mysterious. How does the monarch know just when to leave? How does it find its way through prairies, deserts, valleys, mountains, cities, and neighborhoods? Why do some monarchs migrate, while others do not? Scientists know that monarchs are partly guided by instinct, which acts like an inner map and clock to send the butterflies on their remarkable journeys.

"Monarch" means king or ruler. When butterflies were named, maybe someone thought the monarch's strong wings, brilliant colors, and interesting behavior made it the ruler of butterflies.

CHAPTER ONE:

The monarch is a butterfly, part of a large group of insects. The flashy, orange-and-black monarch belongs to a family of butterflies called milkweed butterflies, so named because they feed on milkweed plants. Milkweed butterflies are some of the largest butterflies in the world.

Like other insects, adult monarchs have six jointed legs, a tough waterproof skin, and three body parts — head, thorax, and abdomen.

The head and body of the monarch are black with white spots. On the butterfly's head are antennae, mouth parts, and eyes. The monarch's two thin, black antennae or feelers end in tiny bent knobs. The monarch feels, tastes, smells, and senses direction with its antennae. The monarch also carries a built-in straw — a long curled tongue called a proboscis (pronounced pruh-BOS-kus). Like other butterflies and moths, the monarch uses its proboscis to suck nectar, a sweet liquid found in flowers.

Monarchs have sharp eyes which help the butterfly spot other monarchs, sense danger, and find sources of food. Human eyes have a single lens. The monarch's two large compound eyes have thousands of lenses. The lenses work together to create a picture. Each lens sees part of the image. The monarch can see color, movement, and shape in all directions except directly

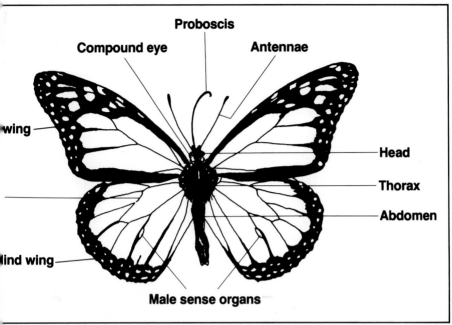

Proboscis

Compound eye

Antennae

wing

Head

Thorax

Abdomen

lind wing

Male sense organs

A male monarch butterfly.

under its body.

The thorax, the middle body part, is the motor which runs the butterfly. Without strong muscles in the thorax, the butterfly couldn't move. Three pairs of legs and two pairs of wings are attached to the thorax.

The monarch's big, bright wings make a beautiful sight as it flits from flower to flower. The wings measure three to four inches (7.6 to 10.1 centimeters) from tip to tip, about the size of the palm of an adult's hand. The wings are the orange color of flames and are lined with black veins and borders. Small white spots dot the borders and upper wings.

Like all butterflies, monarchs have wings made of clear membrane, or soft bendable tissue. Covering the wings are tiny flat scales. The scales are really flattened hairs which give the wings their color. These layered scales help male and female butterflies find each other by sight and smell.

The abdomen is the butterfly's largest and softest body part. It is divided into segments or sections. Tiny holes called spiracles on each segment help the butterfly breathe. The abdomen contains the stomach and the sex organs, and holds the female's eggs until

Tiny flat scales cover a monarch's wings.

they are laid.

The outside of a monarch's body feels hard like a shell. It's made of chitin (pronounced KITE-n), a tough material which protects the organs inside. Unlike humans, butterflies do not have a framework of bones to protect the soft tissues inside. Chitin does this job, forming a firm outer shell called an exoskeleton.

Male monarchs have two black dots on their hind wings which advertise the male's own special perfume. These dots are scent receivers. During mating, these scent receivers act like sponges, absorbing the flowery perfume the male gives off, and later releasing it to attract the female.

An international traveler

Monarchs are international travelers, found from southern Canada to Mexico and South America. Although they once were found only in North America, monarchs have spread into Asia and Australia, the Hawaiian Islands, and parts of Europe.

In North America, monarchs are common from Texas to Minnesota, Georgia to California. When adult monarchs fly, they head for areas with many flowers — grassy fields, quiet roadsides and meadows, yards, parks, and gardens. When mating and laying eggs, monarchs look for areas where milkweed grows.

A powerful flier

The monarch is a powerful flier because of its strong wings and small, light body. Monarchs fly almost all year long in warmer climates. They can travel long distances, some as far as 2,000 miles (3,219 kilometers). Imagine walking 80 miles (129 km). Monarchs can fly that far in a single day!

The long, gently curved wings of the monarch look fragile. But monarch wings have sturdy veins (tiny tubes which pump fluid) which support each wing.

Butterfly wings have built-in propellers and flaps like an airplane. The two pairs of wings work together. The top wings, or forewings, closest to the butterfly's head, help lift the butterfly up into the air and move it forward. They are stiff because of the tightly-packed veins inside. The hind or bottom wings, closest to the abdomen, are more flexible and can bend in flight. The hind wings help the monarch glide, change speed, balance, and steer.

Monarchs fly different ways, depending on whether they are feeding, mating, migrating, or escaping. When monarchs are feeding or flying long distances, they glide. This means they float with wings spread out, fly faster for a while, then return to gliding. With this leisurely combination of gliding and power flying, the monarch flies at about ten miles (16 km) per hour. The broad wings of the monarch work well for gliding. Monarchs would not be able to fly thousands of miles if they had to flap their wings the whole way.

If a monarch is frightened or is escaping from danger, its wings can beat fast. It can fly 20 to 30 miles (32 to 48 km) per hour.

During migration, strong wings carry the monarch thousands of miles.

When a male monarch chases a female, the flight pattern becomes a fast zig-zag as the female tries to get away from the male. The two monarchs fly high in a quick spiraling flight, and return closer to the ground. Some mating flights are fast and short; others are longer.

Monarchs often fly together just to socialize. Sometimes several migrating butterflies will follow each other in a wide circle, cruising and gliding 100 feet (30 meters) in the air. They stay together, drifting with the wind, or circling to greater heights.

CHAPTER TWO:

Milkweed for the caterpillar

The monarch caterpillar is very hungry when it hatches from its tiny egg. Fortunately, the caterpillar's mother laid the egg on the underside of the caterpillar's favorite food—milkweed leaves. The caterpillar spends most of its short life feeding on the leaves, flower buds, and milky juice of the milkweed plant.

The tiny caterpillar eats all during the day and sometimes even at night. Hunger is not the only reason the caterpillar eats. It is storing fat to provide energy for spinning its jewel-like chrysalis and changing into a butterfly.

The caterpillar's body is perfect for heavy-duty eating. On its head are strong jaws for chewing. Other smaller mouthparts help the caterpillar taste, touch, and smell its food. These tiny mouthparts also guide the caterpillar along the plant. A large stomach digests the huge amounts of mashed-up milkweed leaves the caterpillar eats. Eight pairs of legs move the caterpillar to its next milkweed meal.

Monarch caterpillars constantly eat milkweed leaves—they pause only briefly to rest.

13

The Viceroy butterfly is a close lookalike to the monarch butterfly.

Nectar for the adult butterfly

While monarch caterpillars love milkweed leaves, the adult butterflies cannot bite or chew. The adult butterfly uncurls its long, thin proboscis to drink nectar from the flowers of milkweed and other plants.

Adult butterflies also need water to live. They get some water from the liquid nectar in flowers. They can drink from ponds, lakes, or drops of dew or rain. Butterflies also take in moisture through the spiracles, or breathing holes.

Just like many people, butterflies love something sweet. When a monarch lands on a flower, tiny tasters on the butterfly's feet (called tarsi) pick up the sweetness and send a message to the butterfly's brain about how sweet the flower is. A monarch is 2,400 times more sensitive to sweetness than people are. When the butterfly tastes something sweet, its proboscis uncurls, ready to drink.

While butterflies eat, they do an important job. They help pollinate or fertilize flowers. As the monarch drinks nectar, its proboscis and feet brush up against yellow powdery pollen on the flowers. The pollen sticks to the hairs on the butterfly's body. When the monarch visits other flowers, the pollen falls off, fertilizing the plant. Pollination makes it possible for flowers to produce fruits and seeds, and to continue growing.

Milkweed: food and protection

The milkweed plant gives the monarch special protection. Milkweed contains poisons. The caterpillar is immune to the poisons, so it is not harmed by them. But the poisons become part of its body. When the caterpillar turns into a butterfly, the milkweed poisons remain in the body of the butterfly as well.

When a bird tries to eat a monarch, the bird experiences a nasty taste. The butterfly may die, but the bird learns a lesson. When another monarch flutters by, the bird will avoid it just the way people avoid a skunk!

CHAPTER THREE:

Monarchs breed wherever milkweed is plentiful. While monarchs breed all over North America, there are two main breeding groups, one in the east and one in the west. The eastern butterflies migrate from northeastern United States and southern Canada to Florida and other southern states. Many continue south, flying deep into Mexico.

Monarchs migrate south and spend the winter in semi-hibernation.

The other large group of monarchs is found in the western United States, especially the Salinas (pronounced Suh-LEE-nus) and San Joaquin (pronounced San Wa-KEEN) valleys of California and other mountain valleys of the West. The western monarchs migrate to coastal areas between Monterey and Los Angeles, California.

Monarchs leave their northern breeding grounds in late summer or fall and travel south to warmer wintering areas. Usually, one to two generations of monarchs are born in the northern breeding areas, and three to four generations are born in the southern areas or on the way north again. Monarchs born in late summer may not mate until the next spring.

Looking for a mate

The mating of monarchs usually takes place during the spring or summer. An adult male monarch rests in warm open places on the tips of weeds or branches. The male searches for a female that might be drinking nectar from the flowers.

Monarch butterflies use their feet to taste the sweetness of flowers.

The senses of smell and sight are important in helping monarchs find each other. Both sexes spot the familiar patterns formed by the orange, black, and white wing scales. Males have a special scent, which comes from a scent gland at the base of their abdomens. This perfume spills over onto the black scent patches on the male's hind wings. The fragrance is released slowly into the air. When a male brushes up against the lower tip of a female's abdomen, his flowery scent surrounds her.

The chase

What happens next looks like a game of tag. The male and female soar skyward in a fast flight, lasting a few minutes or longer. Back and forth they fly, zig-zagging in the air. Circling round and round each other, they fly straight upward in graceful spirals. They can cover hundreds of yards, and fly hundreds of feet above the earth.

At last, they come to rest on a leaf or branch. The male grabs the female's abdomen with his claspers, two claw-like organs at the tip of his abdomen. If startled, the male is strong enough to carry the female up into the air. Her body hangs beneath him, her legs folded, her wings closed. Flying this way, male and female look like a lovely orange and black flower floating through the air.

The male monarch gives off a perfume from his scent gland that attracts the female.

The pair comes to rest in a protected spot. There, the pair remains linked together for 2 to 14 hours. The male deposits enough sperm in the female's body to fertilize the eggs she will lay. When mating is over, the male flies away to feed and pollinate flowers and to mate again.

The female lays her eggs soon after mating. Searching for just the right milkweed leaf, the female holds her wings high and bends her abdomen in a semi-circle to lay a tiny egg on the fuzzy underside of the leaf. A female monarch can lay as many as 400 eggs in her lifetime. But of those eggs, only a small number grow to become butterflies. Many adult butterflies don't live long enough to migrate and mate. That's why both mating and egg laying are important to the survival of the monarch.

CHAPTER FOUR:

Butterflies and moths change forms four times as they grow. What starts out as a tiny monarch egg on the bottom of a milkweed leaf becomes a fat, creeping caterpillar, then a smooth green chrysalis, and finally a delicate, winged monarch butterfly. This wonderful change of form is called metamorphosis, meaning "many changes."

A female monarch lays her egg on the caterpillar's favorite food — a milkweed leaf.

A tiny green egg

Monarch eggs are tiny, about the size of the head of a pin, and a delicate pale green. The female monarch lays one egg on the underside of each young, tender milkweed leaf. She finds the milkweed by "tasting" the leaves with her feet. She avoids unhealthy plants. They wouldn't be good food for the tiny caterpillars which hatch from her eggs. The female monarch stays away from leaves holding spiders which may eat the eggs. She also avoids leaves where other caterpillars rest, because they could compete for the same food.

In warm weather, the egg grows fast. In three to four days, the caterpillar hatches. As the weather gets cooler in late summer, the egg may take four to six days to hatch.

Not all the eggs laid by the female monarch live. Some eggs fall into water and drown. Other eggs are eaten by insects. And if tiny caterpillars do hatch, they can be gobbled up by small animals or birds. Of every ten eggs laid, just a few will survive and grow.

The larva: an eating machine

Under the milkweed leaf, the tiny monarch caterpillar (the larva stage) chews through the eggshell and crawls out. The caterpillar has a black, bead-like head and a greyish-green body. The first thing the caterpillar does is eat his own eggshell, which is rich in nourishment. Then the caterpillar rests.

At first, the baby caterpillar can only nibble the leaf's fuzzy surface. But after only six hours, the caterpillar is strong enough to start munching on the leaf itself. From then on, the caterpillar becomes an eating machine. It feeds almost constantly, pausing briefly to rest, then feeds again.

As the caterpiller eats, it changes. Its skin darkens and becomes striped with bands of black and yellow. Two pairs of black horn-like stalks poke up into the air at the caterpillar's front and back. The black button which looked like the whole head when the caterpillar hatched now looks like a face mask.

In just three days, the caterpillar doubles its size. By the time the caterpillar is full grown (10 to 20 days, depending on the weather), the caterpillar weighs 2,700 times more than it did as an egg! If a six-pound (2.7-kilogram) human baby ate that much and grew that fast, it would weigh eight tons (7,256 kg) two or three weeks after being born!

The caterpillar's soft body is divided into segments with a hard round head at the front. On the front three segments are three pairs of short bendable legs, called true legs, with sharp claws at the end. These legs help the caterpillar hold on to the leaf. On the middle and back segments are five pairs of legs called false legs, or prolegs. These prolegs, like little suction cups, help the caterpillar cling to smooth surfaces.

The stomach takes up most of the caterpillar's body inside. Strong muscles in the abdomen make the caterpillar's walking prolegs move, and help digest its food.

Close to the caterpillar's strong biting jaws are six simple eyes, so small that the caterpillar can only tell night from day. The caterpillar smells and tastes to find its way to the milkweed plant. Like the adult

After they begin eating, caterpillars double their size in just three days.

To keep from falling, a caterpillar anchors itself to leaves with a silk thread.

butterfly, the caterpillar can taste with its feet. Two short antennae near its jaws help the caterpillar feel its way along the leaves.

Wherever the caterpillar goes, it carries a silky thread, which acts like a safety chain. Through a spinneret, a tiny tube near its jaws, the caterpillar spins a liquid which hardens into a silky thread. The caterpillar anchors itself to each leaf with the silky thread.

The caterpillar keeps eating until its skin is stretched so tight the caterpillar can't eat any more.

A strange thing happens then. The caterpillar's skin splits, uncovering a brand new skin beneath it. This molting of the skin is called an instar.

The molting looks a little like a deep-sea diver unzipping and peeling off a wetsuit. With its two back prolegs, the caterpillar grabs hold of some of the silk it has spun, and pushes forward with all its strength until the skin splits just behind the head and down the back. Over the next three hours, the caterpillar wriggles out of its skin.

Once out of its old skin, the caterpillar can get into trouble. The new skin beneath is soft, and the caterpillar must wait until it hardens. If no enemy looking for a fast meal appears, the caterpillar is safe.

In the next 10 to 20 days, the caterpillar outgrows its skin five times (five instars). The warmer the weather, the faster the caterpillar grows. By the time the caterpillar is ready to spin a chrysalis, it will be plump and almost two inches (5 cm) long.

The pupa: wrapped in green silk

When the caterpillar is 10 to 20 days old, it finally stops eating and looks for a firm leaf, twig, or windowsill. Here the caterpillar spins a pad or button

The caterpillar spins a button of silk, hangs in a "J" shape...

of silk, about the size of a pearl. The caterpillar grabs on to the silk with its back prolegs and hangs upside down in a "J" shape. Then, wriggling hard, the caterpillar sheds its skin for the last time, exposing the

...and sheds its skin at the beginning of the pupa stage.

pupa's body, a shapeless lump splotched with color—
green, white, and yellow—which has been forming
inside the caterpillar. The last thing the caterpillar
does is to attach itself to the silky button by a black

29

The blue-green chrysalis hardens around the monarch pupa.

stalk with hook-like claws (called cremaster) at the tip of its abdomen. Then, as the monarch pupa hangs motionless, its outer skin hardens, wrapping the pupa's body in a hard-shelled, blue-green chrysalis with raised, metallic gold spots. The gold spots control the beautiful colors in the growing butterfly.

After about 15 days, the chrysalis looks like a polished stone.

Inside the mummy-like chrysalis, the caterpillar changes into an adult butterfly. Over the next 12 to 15 days, the body of the caterpillar turns into liquid and the inner organs reorganize. From the liquid, the butterfly grows. At first, the chrysalis looks like a polished jade stone. Toward the end of the pupa stage,

Toward the end of the pupa stage, the monarch butterfly can be seen through the chrysalis.

the chrysalis becomes transparent. The colors, legs, tongue, abdomen, and wings of a grown butterfly show clearly through the filmy chrysalis wall.

Soon the chrysalis wall cracks, and the adult butterfly struggles out. At first, the butterfly is weak and moist. Its wings lie thick and crumpled at its sides. But in just 8 to 20 minutes, the butterfly stretches and spreads its wings. Air and body fluids pump into the limp, fleshy wings. The butterfly flattens its wings, now full size, to dry in the sun. After several hours the adult is ready to fly.

After emerging from the chrysalis, the monarch waits for its wings to dry.

The adult butterfly

The monarch butterfly looks very different from the caterpillar. While the caterpillar's body was soft and worm-like, the adult butterfly's body has a stiff upper skeleton with powerful muscles in its thorax to support its strong wings. Also on the thorax are three pairs of thin legs. The front pair of legs do less of the walking work than the stronger back two pairs.

Since the adult butterfly will live on small amounts of nectar and water, its stomach is small—only one-tenth the size of the caterpillar's. The butterfly now has sensitive antennae and powerful compound eyes.

A quick-change artist

The monarch's remarkable four-stage metamorphosis from tiny egg to grown butterfly takes about five weeks. Monarchs live for only 2 to 12 months.

Compared to humans, the monarch's growth is rapid. With people, it takes 100 years to produce great-great-grandchildren! With several generations of monarchs born in just a few months, it takes less than a year!

CHAPTER FIVE:

If a person makes a 1,000-mile (1,609-km) walking trip, the journey makes the national news. Monarchs quietly make their yearly migration, attracting attention only in the places where huge numbers of them flock together.

Monarch butterflies are migrants, which means they move back and forth from one place to another along special routes. Each year, monarchs fly south along similar paths. In early spring and summer, returning monarchs travel north, with new generations replacing the old.

Flying south to survive

Monarchs can't stay in areas where the temperature falls below freezing. They must migrate south to survive. The monarch has no way to maintain its body temperature the way warm-blooded animals do. If the weather turns cold, the monarch's body temperature will also drop, and the butterfly won't be able to move. On cold mornings, monarchs have to sit in the sun or flap their wings to warm up.

Monarchs begin to move south in the late summer and early fall when many flowers containing nectar are blooming. Some monarchs travel alone or in small groups, but most gather in large clusters of hundreds or thousands. On a fall day in Wisconsin, a pine tree might be changed into a shimmering golden monarch tree by a mass of monarch butterflies clinging to the pine needles.

Butterflies choose trees which have leaves they can grasp with the tiny claws on their feet. That way, even if the butterflies are too cold to move, their feet hold on for them. Favorite trees are willows, pines, and maples in the East, and eucalyptus (pronounced yoo-ka-LIP-tus) and Monterey pines in the West.

Monarchs don't fly at night. During migration, they stop before the sun sets and roost (rest or sleep) in the trees overnight. Monarchs rest with their paired wings folded together. The warm morning sun dries the dew from their wings. Then the flock of thousands lifts swiftly into the air to continue the southward trek.

Monarch flocks often roost in wooded areas near large bodies of water or on peninsulas jutting out from the land toward the south. Some favorite stopping spots are Cape May, New Jersey, the Monterey Peninsula in California, the Gulf Coast, or the Great Lakes. Monarchs also choose trees or bushes near fields, ravines, lakes, rivers, or creeks. Year after year, monarchs stop at the same resting spots even if the butterflies are the offspring of the monarchs who flew south the year before.

Monarchs usually fly close to the ground, about 15

In the early morning, monarchs hold on tightly to leaves and branches until their wings are warm enough to fly.

feet (4.5 m) high. But they can soar to great heights over forests, buildings, or mountain ridges. Monarchs have been found in mountain ranges at 11,000 feet (3,353 m) above sea level. Migrating monarchs fly in a diagonal pattern, from northeast to southwest.

A place to spend the winter

Monarchs search for a cozy tree to settle down in for the winter. Monarchs move south until early

Migrating monarchs cover trees, their trunks, and the ground!

October, when groups reach Florida or the mountains of central and southern Mexico in the East and between San Francisco and Los Angeles along the coast of southern California in the West. Other wintering sites are the Atlantic coast of Georgia and Florida, the Gulf Coast from Florida to Mexico, and the Pacific coast of Mexico.

Monarchs live through the winter in small groups or in large clusters on well-protected trees. Most monarchs spend the winter in a state of semi-hibernation, which means their bodies slow down into a resting state. If the days grow warm, the wintering monarchs may leave the tree briefly, flutter around a little, and return to the tree. But most of the time they quietly hang on the tree. Their lack of motion helps the butterflies store up fat which will give them energy for the return trip north.

With thousands of monarchs hanging from their branches, the trees look blanketed in pale orange and black leaves. With wings folded together, the monarchs rest motionless except for an occasional breeze rustling their wings. In one main wintering spot in Sierra Madre, Mexico, a scientist discovered a mountain clearing carpeted with millions of monarchs. The butterflies covered at least a thousand trees, their trunks, and the ground.

When monarchs are in semi-hibernation, they do not mate until just before they migrate northward in the spring. Some monarchs do not go into semi-hibernation, but breed and stay in the South through several generations.

The trip back north

As spring nears, the monarchs grow restless. Instinct tells the butterflies it's time to move north. Scientists think it may have something to do with the angle of the sun. But somehow, the monarchs know it's time to begin the hard journey. Some of the original migrants may travel with them. The rest of the travelers are offspring of the butterflies who migrated south.

Some monarchs mate before flying north. Then they leave, alone or in groups, flying at speeds of 10 to 30 miles (32 to 48 km) per hour. A flock of monarchs lifting into the sky makes a blizzard of fluttering orange and black wings.

Migrating monarchs face the danger of below-freezing temperatures common in spring and early summer. Or, if the weather suddenly turns warm, the butterflies may fly too far north, only to be trapped in below-freezing air.

The monarchs who flutter into the meadows of the North in early summer may be the great-great-grandchildren of the adult butterflies who left there the fall before. People in the South may spot monarchs

To learn more about monarchs, scientists tag butterflies and track their movements.

in March and April, those in the Midwest in April and May, the North in May and June.

Tracking the monarch

Tagging monarchs helps people learn more about the butterflies' remarkable journey. Entomologists (pronounced ent-uh-MAHL-uh-gists), scientists who study insects, know a great deal about monarchs. But to learn more about where monarchs fly, scientists have tagged (marked the wings of) thousands of monarchs. Scientists gently scrape off a few of the butterfly's scales, and press on a lightweight sticky tab. The tab stays on the butterfly but does not hurt it. Although it is difficult to keep track of so many tagged butterflies, entomologists have found butter-flies in Mexico that could have been tagged in Minnesota. A butterfly tagged in Mexico may be sighted in Texas, 1,000 miles (1,609 km) away. Others make it all the way back to Canada.

CHAPTER SIX:

Monarchs and weather

Weather affects the monarch's growth. Rain can drown a caterpillar. Cold weather late in the summer can slow the pupa's growth so that the adult butterfly starts south too late to avoid early winter blizzards.

Weather is hard on migrating monarchs. Even though monarchs won't fly in rain, violent rain and wind storms still kill thousands of monarchs.

Monarchs usually avoid flying over large bodies of water. Flying over land, butterflies can always rest. Over water, a sudden wind gust can toss them into the water. Of the millions of monarchs who begin the trip south, many die on the way.

The monarch's enemies

The monarch has fewer enemies than many insects, but there are some. The tachinid (pronounced TAK-uh-nud) fly occasionally lays its egg on the body of the monarch caterpillar. When the egg hatches, the tachinid larva burrows into the caterpillar and eats the caterpillar from the inside out. Ground beetles, ants, or animals also may prey on the tiny caterpillar.

When some monarch caterpillars sense danger, they curl up in a ball and drop to the ground. Then they lie motionless, hidden among grasses and weeds, until danger passes. If the caterpillar is lucky, it will find its way back to the milkweed plant.

If a newly-hatched monarch butterfly falls to the ground before its wings have time to dry, it can be attacked by ants, mice, toads, or shrews. But thanks to the poisons in the milkweed plant, the butterfly is protected from most birds.

Monarchs and humans

Monarchs depend on milkweed. As more and more people move into the country where monarchs live, it may mean danger for the monarch. If the meadows disappear, monarchs must search elsewhere for milkweed.

Monarchs also need protected trees to roost in during migration or to use as their winter homes. Whole forests of trees are often cut down to make room for new houses. Even so, as the areas where monarchs live become more crowded, scientists hope there will always be room for this magnificent insect.

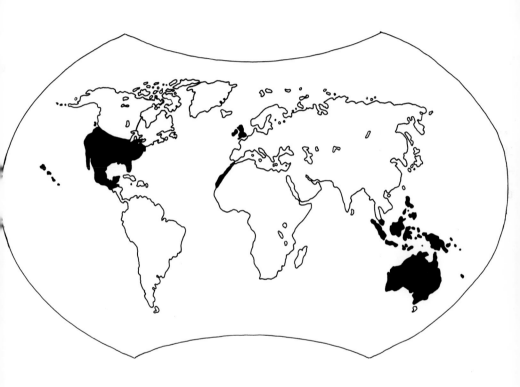

Most monarchs live within these areas.

INDEX/GLOSSARY:

Sweet liquid produced by flowers and drunk by butterflies.

PROBOSCIS 6, 15—*Long, coiled tube through which a butterfly sucks its food.*

PROLEGS 24, 27, 28—*Short, stubby legs. On the caterpillar, prolegs are the back five pairs of legs. Suction cups at the ends help caterpillars hold on to smooth, slippery surfaces.*

PUPA 5, 27, 29, 30, 31, 42—*The stage of growth when a caterpillar changes into an adult butterfly inside the hard-shelled chrysalis.*

SCALE 8—*One of the small, thin, flattened hairs that overlap on the butterfly's wings to create their brilliant colors.*

SEMI-HIBERNATION 39—*Inactive resting state. During*

their winter state of semi-hibernation, most monarchs store fat for energy for the return trip northward.

SIMPLE EYES 24—*Eyes that have only one lens.*

SPERM 21—*The male reproductive cell needed to produce young caterpillars.*

SPIRACLES 8, 15—*Pairs of openings on each segment of the abdomen which help the caterpillar and butterfly breathe and take in moisture.*

THORAX 6, 7, 34—*The center or middle part of an insect's body, containing legs and wings.*

VEINS 7, 10—*Tiny tubes to carry fluid inside an animal's body. Veins form a framework for the butterfly's wings.*

WILDLIFE
HABITS & HABITAT

READ AND ENJOY THE SERIES:

If you would like to know more about all kinds of wildlife, you should take a look at the other books in this series.

You'll find books on bald eagles and other birds. Books on alligators and other reptiles. There are books about deer and other big-game animals. And there are books about sharks and other creatures that live in the ocean.

In all of the books you will learn that life in the wild is not easy. But you will also learn what people can do to help wildlife survive. So read on!